A Hundred of Happiness
and Other Poems

Martin Stannard

Smith/Doorstop Books

Published 1995 by
Smith/Doorstop Books
The Poetry Business
The Studio
Byram Arcade
Westgate
Huddersfield HD1 1ND

Copyright © Martin Stannard 1995
All Rights Reserved

ISBN 1 869961 55 2

British Library Cataloguing-in-Publication Data. A catalogue entry for this book is available from the British Library.

Typeset at The Poetry Business in 10.5pt Garamond
Printed by Swiftprint, Huddersfield

Cover by the blue door design company, adapted from 'My Week' (reduction linoprint) by Dale Devereux Barker, 1991.

Distributed by Password (Books) Ltd.,
23 New Mount Street, Manchester M4 4DE

The Poetry Business gratefully acknowledges the help of Kirklees Metropolitan Council and Yorkshire & Humberside Arts.

Thanks are due to the editors of the following magazines where some of these poems, or slightly different versions of them, first appeared:
Ambit; Joe Soap's Canoe; Odyssey; Oasis; Rustic Rub; Scratch; Slow Dancer; Tears in the Fence; Terrible Work; The Echo Room; The North; The Rialto; The Wide Skirt; Uncompromising Positions
"You'd Be Better off Dead" was first published in *Jewels & Binoculars* (Stride/Westwords, 1993)
"From A Recluse To A Roving I Will Go" was first published as a hand-printed limited edition book in collaboration with printmaker Dale Devereux Barker (The Shed, Ipswich 1992)

CONTENTS

5	Euclid Avenue
7	In Air the Romans Breathed
9	The Beloved
10	The Expected
11	The Coma
12	The Treasure
13	The Inheritance
14	The Island
15	Evidence
17	Stuff I Knew
19	A Thin White Man
20	The Surface under Glass
22	Hot News from a Cold Place
23	The Real New Criticism
24	Bliss
27	From a Recluse to a Roving I Will Go
34	His Story
36	Guide
38	A Hundred of Happiness
39	Pick of the Films
41	How to Approach a Poem
42	Christmas
43	Yes
44	Against Madness
46	Five Poems
49	Poem of Carelessness
50	The Secret
51	Noticing the Wallpaper
52	The Other Position
54	You'd be Better Off Dead
56	The First and the Last Attempt
57	Lies I Must Remember
58	The Wit and Wisdom of Barney Ambrose
60	Adventures with Everything

61 Where Bears Walk
63 Prince and Princess of Hats
64 Sense of a Horse
65 Reading the Poem
66 How I Measure Other People's Lives
67 Looking at Maps
68 Book
69 Life of Fish
70 Punish
71 The Aeroplane

Euclid Avenue

Anna Angeletti hires a piano
to satisfy the peculiar demands
of the visitors from England.

Stars are shining brightly
as a desperate Keats
tries to finish "Death On The Piazza"
and comes up instead with Chapter 9
of *The Boy's Book of Myths*.

Life, for some people, is not special. Advice:

"If you're going to identify with characters
in the books you read
be careful what you read."

The crescent moon
catches a gleam of red sky
and someone is doing the monthly accounts
to avoid reading
some dull poetry. Tell me,

do you think
My Tedious Life
is a good title
for a book?

It's been used before
but a long time ago
and what Keats said
about filling some other body
reminds me I have a job to go to.

In some parts of the world
people believe that doing nothing

is the same as being everything;
in other parts of the world
people believe that life is all
steady progress toward death.

Let's face it,
if clarity is what you seek
you are not going to find this
kind of stuff very helpful.

Here on Euclid Avenue
a fantastic bird of many colours
has every question and every answer
but is having trouble matching them up.

The houses are brilliant
and have all we're ever going to need
but living in them
is a trial.

In Air the Romans Breathed

Sound of approaching invalid carriage
Sound of invalid carriage fading into neighbouring distance.

The lamplight's in the window across the street
And all the old stand-bys are brought into play:
When desperate, act with desperation.
Nobody'll mind because nobody gives a damn.

Someone dead, benign and influential:
Hey, buck up!
The Complete Poems of John Wilmot, Earl of Rochester
Okay, Frank. I'll buck up. At least, I'll try.

A man who spends his life on his knees
Is searching the store for a table lamp, and it's
Very important the children grow up in our image.

Look of reproach in rear view mirror
Look of me and you in rear view mirror.
Wardrobe of the doomed in spare bedroom.

Men are boys.   The empty car park .

Nobody knows if you're coming or going but
They know your name. So, what's your name?
The forest is ever nearing your little house.

The forest is swallowing our little house
And I'm afraid nobody'll notice. Sound of party
In neighbouring ranch-style mansionette
Sound of wild party animals trampling fitted prairie carpet
Sound of bomb squad come to close down the eternal barbecue.
Light in the window across the street goes out

And a face replaces it: I know I'm making a small noise,
I'm sorry I'm making a small noise, I'll try
Not to make such a small noise in future.

The Beloved

If you've got something to say to me
then put it in a letter. Trust that I don't
adopt Coleridge's mode of dealing with an extensive
correspondence: open none, answer none.
Anyway, let me tell you,
our kid got snagged on the barbed wire and
since then things here have been pretty hectic,
too pretty hectic for me
to take any notice of stuff coming in from without.
Have you ever seen
the damage barbed wire can do?
George said once he had a really great sheep
skin ripped to shreds out near Polstead. Anyway,
the doll's hospital, which is all we have here,
couldn't cope.
What's that you flash across
Constable Country at me from your point of vantage
using a bit of broken mirror to throw glints
of sun, resourceful as ever?
"Help. Am caught in elephant trap, I mean elegant trap
of eloquent domesticity. Have also lost
all those cassettes you recorded for me."
Okay. I'll sing for you. Listen:
I think our postmen are terrific but misguided.
I want our kid to be a thug.

The Expected

I had this dead crap dream about 'The Dangling Judge'
and coming away with $7\frac{1}{2}$ years for GBH Section 18 then
jerked out of stupor
there's a monk at the door:
"I want to see you".
Oh, The Unexpected. But
it's good, my dad says, to jolt awake the intellect
with an electric shock.
Quite.
Curiosity is a pleasure. Look at today.
Engulfing moon eyes in The Snappy Shopper, bacon
untouched by a lovely lovely girl but
do not disturb the cashier her
life's a mess. Next,
tears in the pub,
drunk in the off-licence pocketing a can of beer.
Interesting and uninteresting people trample
through my life as if they owned the carpet.
My footsteps aren't my own. Look,
there's plenty other pavements in the city,
and we're going to build walls round everything
like in the old days. Empires
can be rebuilt. That's what worries me.

The Coma

Clambered out of the bunk this morning
delighted by the cartoon blue sky and the idea
of small animals in careless hibernation.
Oh, this lavatory-brained world! You know,
those huge buildings made of glass & Meccano
are full of wrong ideas. To some people,
wisdom is a disease, and they call in the fear-squad
when they bump up against a wise man.
Today, with things frozen and still,
there were a few words of love,
but a few words of love usually make me sick.
Here's the map of our souls,
and our reflections in the mirror resembling cauliflowers,
life-forms you think you have nothing in common with
until you get chatting to them. There are things
you don't know until you're on your back
looking up at them through the bloody eyes
of some poor casualty. And this morning
as Nature did what it does outside the window
we coma'd together as we do.

The Treasure

Ice on the cars, European
sailing ships stranded on the solid sea. We
should ride into town (exquisite nobles
on exquisite horseback). January's hard colour.
Beggars under OFFICES TO LET signs, and a browse in
'The Treasure Chest' (2nd hnd bks)
where foreign towers loom
behind pearled skies, and the smell of people.
Sleepiness when the invisible sun is
at its highest, an inability
to do anything at all significant these days.
Ice turned to water, sailing ships
edging toward the continent and
into harbour where children up to their waists in mud
scavenge among sailors' waste, industrial
discards, lost love, treasure
to take home or to sell.
Walking past houses where comfort is measured
by the quality of light,
the solidity of warmth.
Dusk's umbrella descending, closing.
All was supposed to be organised
and all is nothing but a jumble.

The Inheritance

The theatres are impersonal and expensive,
rail terminals are dangerous places after dark.
Bankers hoard such immense wealth
men look up to them as Gods. But,
as the Gods deserved adulation not always, so too
these men of whatever it is, wherever it was,
how it is now.
When maps are delivered
receive them with grace.
The whisper of the ocean is behind each sacred moment;
when heroes depart for another country only the song
    of solemn men remains.
Take care not to inherit inertia before your time.
Remember how much you forget each day:
the name of that man, what was it?
The cost of that meal, what? The books
on those shelves, did you read them?

The Island

Romance of the sea, all at sea;
bloke at the bar telling us about fingers of rum
but there's a pile of laundry at home needs excavating
and pressed into shape. I can't wait. And
so here we are, the body beautiful and the body intolerable,
and how some people reach such positions
of undeserved power beats me. What do you mean, "Vote"?
Waves lap a lapidary shore.
Sailing ships ignorant in the distance
of the suffering,
and all of us ignoring nearby. Our friends
have had a son, and apropos nothing
we should keep filled
the stone pond even in January.
It's a chore but a responsibility. Sometimes I regret
my lack of a classical education, but most times I figure
what the hell. I'm reading
From Popular to Elitist, a dim book
in the fireside armchair. Some
things remain solid: Mark calls in the evening,
broken words from New Jersey on
a mobile phone; the State of the Nation;
then there's my secretary bird, and
gulls swooping above a desert island. Let me
have your list of people to strand on it.

Evidence

Item: he fell from the horse as gun music
filtered through the walls of the empty butterfly
enclosure. Eyewitnesses said the fall was
graceless, a sack of beans being tipped off
the back of a truck on to the warehouse floor.

We are left to ponder a few things
between the departure of the ambulance
for the infirmary and the arrival of the wine
from the songster vineyards of Bulgaria:

Item: who was that ugly bloke seen leaving the vicarage,
a chorister under each arm? Corky McCorcindale said that he
looked like the man on page 137 of Agatha Christie's
The Murder of Roger Ackroyd.

Item: the question mark hanging
over the authenticity of the alleged cloud
seen swallowing the sunlight of the dale.

Item: 49 out of 51, which is an overwhelming majority.

Item: the harmony of a little stream of incessant goodbyes.

Item: the indiscretion of being
caught outside Arturo's Dancette arm-in-arm.

Item: her dress
described by those who saw it
as "greenfinch blue".

Item: all the things I enjoy these days only stir up guilt.

Item: from left to right in the photograph: Malcolm Innes,
sales representative from The Eastern Press Company, Mr
Alan Huffey of The News Shop, and Mrs Pearl Gibson of
Wilberforce Street, winner of Sebastian the Giant Musical
Teddy Bear.

Item: look, I don't want to
rummage in his room while he's away.

Item: the suspicious patrol car music,
and Officers Smith and Wesson "off duty forever".

Item: it'd be ungallant to take advantage of his accident
even though I think he's the collective arsehole of a
thousand flying pigs.

Item: I cannot be a juggler of lives.

Item: if all the world's a stage
then it's decent to be on it,
eating the dust of travel.

Item: eye witness accounts of flight and escape.

Item: 'The Problem Symphony', and its lack of a tune.

Item: The legion dancers of the rodeo,
and the vultures
waiting on the branches of the trees.

Item: *The Science of Luck* (2 vols.) by Egil Skallagrimsson.

Item: the mad horse has become a folk hero more great
than The Window Cleaner in The Bank of Evening.

Item: the sadness of the departure lounge.

Item: Absence was summoned, ladies and gentlemen,
and, as usual, has proved his guilt by not showing up.

Stuff I Knew

I knew she had been seeing someone
else but I gave her the car keys
anyway. I knew God was dead but I
still sent him a Valentine's card.
I knew what happiness was but I
couldn't let that get me down.
I knew my future was behind me
but I set to the task body and
soul. I knew people misunderstood
but I'd always wanted to be popular
and much-loved. I knew the fat was a
flame but I had immense faith in the fire
brigade. I knew the roads were bad but
my aeroplane was in the hangar having
its wings fixed. I knew Ernest
Hemingway was a great novelist
but still thought his books stank.
I knew my parents were not made of
stone but I was never able to get
blood out of them. I knew George
had his problems but I was sure mine
were worse. I knew I wasn't going to get
to heaven but I went for the interview
with an open mind and my life
laid out on a plate. I knew
I was on Dead-end Avenue with no
hope of reprieve but you had to
see the funny side. I knew they were
going to repossess everything but
none of it was mine so what the hell.
I knew my attitude was not good
but I also knew people who
admired my style. Also I knew
the habit was a killer but you

only live once. I knew the lorry
was headed for me but I took
no evasive action. I knew it was
a mistake because I knew a mistake
when I saw one, I'd seen so many.

A Thin White Man

        Night and its black sky
and white snow is falling. You can't
see the road, but the middle of the field
has just smacked you on the nose. A
sense of direction is a wonderful thing,
if you are the sort of man who can find
one. Wet rain lands on the hat on your
head and you can count the drops as they
fall: one, seven, four, nine. Watching
your watch (lucky it has a luminous
dial!) you observe time casually
pass you by. You can count the seconds,
and even the years: four, nineteen,
forty-two, four again. A man walks
his black dog in the black night
and they leave a trail of holes
in the white snow. The field is dark,
and you don't expect it to brighten up
just because dawn's coming. Thunder
and lightning are forecast and sadness
can be depended upon. One moment
in this life it snows, then it rains,
then it snows again. Life's like that,
and can be trusted to stay like that.
Darkness blanks out any light there
may have been. A thin white man
in snow may or may not be invisible,
but he is quiet. Listen: Nothing.

The Surface under Glass

Some things you should not touch:
an elephant apoplexied beyond recall,
for instance, or an airplane so many
leagues under the sea that it is
further than your imagination's range.
A furious mother is another,
and misplaced arrows are even more.
Faces turned inwards, idle hands held
behind the back, observation posts
manned by imbecile boys, a loser's
wager, ponderous offspring of men
carved out of dead trees, these also
are some of the things you should not
touch. You should not touch aristocrats
(though you may take any money they
have on them), nor should you touch
churchmen and members of private clubs;
green and red are colours you should
not touch, and the numbers forty-two
and 31. The sun when it is just risen,
the sun when it is just set, and all
other unbelievably hot things. Also, a
juggler in mid-juggle. A liar in mid-
lie. An ocean liner so far up in
the sky that clouds obscure the
Plimsoll Line. Another thing you
should not touch is a mountain when
it is moving, since this means that
times and all omens are bad. A gun
found in long grass you should not
touch, nor manacles upon a severed
limb. A fallow field, virgin soil,
these should not be touched. A verb
in the middle of its doing, an
adjective in the middle of its

description, and workmen at lunch,
these should not be touched. Father
burning his mouth in fury, anger
turning into iron, love melting into
uselessness, these also should not
be touched. And then the heart. Song
of the open door, the dream of
impossible wealth, dust on dreams,
and a dream house, these should not
be touched. Furthermore, the diamond
of night, the blood in the water,
the minute hand and the second chance,
and a crown on a fool's head. Further:
skin, flesh, hide, and the already
mentioned heart. These are some of
the things that should not be touched.

Hot News from a Cold Place

Bernie Winters is dead and Lennie Summers is in mourning.
Nobody has written an obituary for Bernie Winters, tears
And laughter, and Lennie Summers is in mourning. There is
Not going to be a Bernie Winters retrospective on TV and
Lennie Summers is in mourning. They're not repeating even
One of the *Tonight with Bernie Winters* TV shows and Lennie
Summers is in mourning. Bernie Winters had a brother,
The closeness of family, and Lennie Summers is in mourning.
My Life With Bernie Winters is out of print and Lennie
Summers is in mourning. Bernie Winters is dead,
And Johnny Thunders, and the world of variety substantially
Diminished, and Lennie Summers is in mourning.
Man of Laughter, Man of Tears will not now be made,
Bernie Winters is dead, and Lennie Summers is in mourning.
Corridors to possible worlds, the smiling variety, Bernie
Winters, and Lennie Summers is in mourning. No more
A million smiles, Bernie Winters, worry hardly at all,
And Lennie Summers is in mourning. *My 500 Best Gags* by Bernie
Winters, seasons are passing, time flieth like an arrow by day
Through sunlight and cloud and imagination and Lennie Summers
Is in mourning. Bernie Winters is dead, doors closing doors
Opening, and Lennie Summers is in mourning. Bernie Winters.

The Real New Criticism

So we moved to the Isle of Wight
With a case of un-read books,
A box of matches and a pack of
Firelighters. We knew everything
There was to know about aggression
And were very aggressive. I had
A brand new Sekonda watch,
You wore a fragrance called "Distance".
I said "Art" was about precisely that, and
Sea breaking upon an undiscovered shore.
I opened the case of books and
The odour of a disappearing world
Punched me 'Biff!' on the nose.
I felt sick, I had more important
Things to say and struck a match.
The books burned like bloody fuck.

"Those books burned like bloody fuck,"
You said, as we lay in the after-
Glow of brief sexual intercourse.
"Art is redundant these days, and TV
Is real communication." I got out
Of bed and put on my new Doc Marten's
And you got out of bed and put on
An MC Hammer LP. "We didn't need
The firelighters," I said. "But we might,"
You said. "Yes, you're right."
"I'm always right." "Not always."
"Fucking am." "Fucking aren't."
"Bollocks." "Fuck off." "Fuck you."

Bliss

for Rebecca & Dale

The Wedding-Guest has been duped.
Everybody's duped by the glittering eye:
What they said would never happen has happened,
What they said would happen has not happened.
You can't trust anybody these days:
These days what people say
Isn't worth the paper it's written on.
Even the paper isn't as good as it used to be.
You used to be able to trust paper.
In those days you could trust paper,
You could trust ink,
You could trust a man's dark and doleful moods,
You could trust the poet's tongue
And you could trust the sound of music.
The bassoon would play,
The Wedding-Guest would beat his breast,
And someone would remind someone else that
You only in those days had to talk to a girl six times
And they made you marry her. Great days.
Great days and great ways.
Something to believe in: The Great
Chain of Being and the Music of the Spheres.
Cherubim, Seraphim, no mention
Of credit cards, and women were angels though
Wedlock was the Devil. Great days those days,
But it's not good to cast longing looks
Backwards lingeringly though enjoyment should be
Grasped when seen, for it is but fleeting.
We drive faster but don't get there any quicker.
A man used to be able to trust his horse.
Now he doesn't have a horse, and the Wedding-Guest,
Standing still, says Progress is not moving forward.
Don't look at me like that.

Promises made under duress aren't real promises.
I know how big your brother is. In
My day brothers were even bigger
And didn't need machetes or machine guns.
Don't talk to me about courage.
Okay. You can talk to me about courage
If I can talk to you about cowardice.
All tragedies are finish'd by a death.
Byron said that.
All comedies are ended by a marriage.
Byron said that also.
The most happy marriage I can picture
Or imagine to myself would be
The union of a deaf man to a blind woman.
Coleridge said that.

I know you own the corner shop. I want to see
The accounts. You have to talk about money.
If we don't talk about money now
It'll be too late and it'll be
All there is to talk about. Silence
Embraces us so suddenly. The Wedding-Guest
Sits still on the stone.
Once upon a time you could trust a stone.
In those days you could trust stone,
You could trust the weight round your neck,
You could trust your neck on the block,
You could trust life to be a story
Barely worth the telling,
The story to have a beginning
A middle and an end, and the end to be happy
Or miserable and most probably in hospital.
Now you don't know. Nobody knows anything
Any more. There's so much to know
And it's too much and nobody knows
Nothing. Look at us. We wanted to be

Together. God knows nothing
Any more and he never knew why
We wanted to be together. We read
Lolita,
The Tempest, and
Remembrance of Things Past
In bed,
In deckchairs in bed,
In silence in bed,
In exotic clothing in bed,
In desperation in bed,
And in the end our eyes went. Our eyes went,
Our hair fell out, our limbs atrophied
And our tongues turned to leather.
But we had the kids. The kids were the Sun,
The Moon, the unending voice of the ocean
And its whisperings of eternity,
And a drain on our limited resources.
We had the photographs of the Big Day,
Of the numerous Bad Days,
And of days with far too many hours in them.
The Wedding-Guest turned from the bridegroom's door
And was hit by a truck. In those days
We were happy and innocent,
Now we are more sad, more wise.
The Wedding-Guest died, and we went to his funeral.
It made us think of our place in
The World, the State of the World,
The End of the World, and I
Couldn't be sure I'd turned off the gas.
I kind of hoped I hadn't.

From a Recluse to a Roving I Will Go

First version of first story:
Title: *A Recluse's Life Is Okay By Me.*
Opening scene: stone-wrenching wind,
Moaning of forlorn and lost sheep,
Bewilderment in urban landscape,
Clouds cloaked across vengeful sky,
Firewood soaked by afternoon rains.
Pile of unopened mail on oak table,
Telephone ringing going unanswered.
Damn well didn't ask to be born,
The future ill-starred,
Past beyond remembrance,
Footsteps coming downstairs heavy.
Cup of coffee in kitchen,
Piles of laundry in each corner,
Applications for work abroad,
Photographs of unlikely women,
Clothes by *Man of Our Time*,
Books by unpronounceable East Europeans,
Estimates for car repairs heartbreaking.
Silence in dark moments at noon,
Friends laughing in other towns,
Milk turned in the refrigerator,
Nothing after life but death,
Nothing interesting to say about death,
Time flieth like an arrow,
Everything has a name except this,
Except this useless emotion.
Anger flaring into brilliance,
Frustration splintering like ice,
Life's little loops,
Life's stupid ironies,
Life's comic cuts,

Life's dead ends,
Life's open heart surgeries,
Life's great chip shop closed when you're hungry.
Favourite colour - green,
Favourite food - green,
Colour of jealousy and envy - green.
Visit from incompetent doctor,
Rain lashing against glass,
Power cut thanks to poor government.
Omens bad,
Tempers worse.
Blood oozing from bank statement,
White linen in neat folds on bed,
Wood shavings in carpet slippers,
Hay in the bed,
Silence in the bed,
Wallpaper on the outside walls,
An American prairie in the bed,
Silent moon at dawn,
Anagrams in breakfast cereal.
Dream,
Nightmare,
Fantasy,
Imagination,
Delusion,
Flight of fantastic Lagoon Bird.
Bawling of infant lungs,
Choir of angels,
Hint of Mr. Cleaver, Family Butcher,
The agony and the ecstasy,
The book of the film,
Translations into several languages,
Oceans breaking on a thousand shores,
Innocence and guilt and ignorance,
Week's wages on a useless horse,

Year's salary on a useless quest,
Sleep of the supine,
Kiss of the dead,
Love of the musically illiterate,
Love of the visually illiterate,
Love of the literally illiterate,
The last man out of here won't get out of here alive,
Uselessness of any word,
Speechless in the stained glass of night.

*

Second scene: morning:
Pigs lost in fog,
Postman found murdered in lane,
Bad news from army cousin in Ireland,
Cat hanging from tree,
Midwife mumbling unintelligibly,
Smoke curling from pile of smouldering smocks,
Hollering from crib,
Wife still refusing to enter the action.
Dawn's despair,
Breakfast blend in the coffee machine,
Detectives in the shrubbery.
Evidence of illegal entry,
Footsteps on rained on concrete,
Shadows on private life,
Hat missing from head in mirror,
Bulb missing from light in bathroom,
Sense missing from every waking moment,
Misunderstanding of Euclid's chief theories,
Incomprehension of looking on beauty bare,
Television covered in dust,
Power restored at nine,
Prayers rising into gloomy sky,

Religion lost and found and lost again,
Stranger in the house,
Realisation that life is now changed a lot.

*

Statement from the Divinity: "Life's great."

*

Swine found impersonating tramps on motorway,
Interrogation of swine,
Arrest of swine for murder of postman,
Passing of law forbidding persecution of swine,
Swine released pending public enquiry,
Child utters first words,
First words are either pig, pug, or rugby club.
Bedclothes steaming,
Recollection that something is forgotten,
Books burning in supermarket trolley in garden,
Someone reminds someone of someone else,
The wide world,
The far distance,
Pile of unopened mail covering hall floor,
Telephone disconnected as bill unpaid,
Grandparents arrive from Scotland,
Complaints Department opened in guest bedroom,
Blood and dirt under fingernails,
Holidays on South Coast recalled,
Iron filings under pillow,
Orange turning green in fruit bowl,
Cat turning green in tree,
Lagoon Bird takes flight for China,
Unreal women and urgent imagination,

Selected Cantos of Ezra Pound
Two hours sleep in last thirty-six hours,
One moment of peace scheduled in next twenty years.
Pink sky of early evening,
Empire of declining influences,
Silence and beer,
Optimism and despair,
Eyes cloaked in layers of skin and loathing,
Misunderstanding of notion of responsibility,
Clarity like a bell cracking the silence,
Innocence in white,
Guilt in black,
Misinterpreted sense of humour,
Sense of self,
Sense of life,
Sense of what is nonsense.

*

Fourth scene, third missing, similar story:
Title: *Will I Ever Get To Go A Roving?*
Closing scene:
Forlorn and moaning lost souls,
Bewildered and urban,
Longing for escape,
Wrapped in cloak of solitude,
Afternoon pain lasting into middle of next week,
Weeks running into months and years,
Men running into mists of unreal women,
Men running into oblivion off high cliffs,
Men running into old friends in graveyards,
Men running into trouble,
Men running into brick walls,
Men running into the distance,
The distance nearing,

Men running blindly into it.
Men becoming consumed with misunderstandings.
Men becoming consumed by all-consuming passions.
Men becoming consumed by mistakes.
Men becoming consumed with evening meal.
Men honing art of self-pity to perfection,
Men taking imaginary burden to Olympian heights.
Floorboards curling in damp of autumn,
Paint peeling off prow of ship,
House falling down around ears,
Oil dripping from sump to tarmac,
Leaves dropping from boughs to green green grass,
Socks turning into soil in composted corners,
A different government,
The same balls up,
Refusal to listen to screams in night's deep,
Option of opting out refused and refused,
You didn't ask to be born,
Dogs barking in murmuring backyards,
Neighbours hanging baskets from caravans,
Old man sweeping lawn with ragged cardigan,
Rust flaking from combine harvester,
Ocean lapping at doorstep,
School closed,
Shops to let,
Pavements cracked,
Railway abandoned,
Man falls off ship into dock and never seen no more,
Bus late,
Factory derelict,
Bank collapsed,
Didn't have no money in it anyway,
Police corrupt,
Church corrupt,
Government corrupt,
Car fucked,

Evergreens no longer able to inspire sense of rhapsody,
Pissed off with career,
Someone calling name from kitchen,
Someone calling name from distant village,
Someone calling name from frozen bed,
Someone calling name from serious balcony,
Someone calling name from patio,
Someone calling name from shrubbery (The Fanny Price Walk),
Someone calling name from blackest night,
Someone calling name from abandoned restaurant,
Someone calling name from brilliant farm,
Someone calling name from *The Sunday Times Atlas of the World*.
Hang it all,
If you don't study, that's your fault.
Never had any ambition,
Had nothing to say,
Could say nothing,
Grew hysterical,
Grew hot,
Grew cold,
Grew indifferent,
Stopped growing.
Come home from work, house is gone.
Come home from work, family's gone.
Come home from work, want to go back to work.
Come home from work, God is dead.
Hang it all.
Hang it all and hang it all.

His Story

If you insist I tell the truth, I went to sea to flee my family. Living in that ramshackle house by the harbour was getting me down. Okay, I didn't give much thought, any thought at all, to whether or not it was getting my wife and kids down too. She had her part-time job cleaning at the inn, and the kids seemed to delight everyone, everyone except me, that is. I'd see the boats and the ships, and hear the sailors talk about this, that and the other, and their words were like flowers in a wilderness, the ocean a magnet to my iron heart. Any road, I did it on the spur of the moment, sort of, even though I'd been thinking about it for ages. "The Angel" was bound for Bombay, I'd had a bit too much to drink perhaps, and no, I didn't say Goodbye and thinking about it now fair wrecks my head. But what's done is done and it can't be undone. I don't know if I can ever go back. Since I've been at sea I've changed a lot and the people who knew me back then probably wouldn't know me now even if they had a mind to. I read a lot, and I've thought long and hard, and I've learned that unto the pure all things are pure, but I don't know where that leaves me. Gertrude Stein said that a rogue is a rogue is a rogue, but I swear that now my intentions are honourable and my ends of the most admirable. There is a prayer –

"Lord,
May the Sky
Be constant azure overhead,
And the Ocean a murmuring
Never melancholy friend;
To all good wishes allow
A flowering of fulfilment.
May Comradeship, Loyalty,
Love and Compassion
Be our guides to the edges

Of the discovered world.
May we bear Tempest,
Storm, Disease and Trial
With strength and dignity,
And should Evil threaten
Our bow give us spines
Of tempered steel.
We give ourselves
To you, Lord."

– and The Bible bids us pray without ceasing. I do what I can. I used to wish that the cabin boy would beg to share my bed and turn out to be a girl, but no more. I pray that my life be transformed into a neural calm, and that I be granted amiable and rewarding converse with wave and star, that a mild acceptance grace my every breath. I already accept the existence of miracles in this world.

Guide

From the War Memorial take the lane
past the vicarage and the abandoned orphanage.
Continue along until the municipal car park
is at your elbow. If the wind is from the East
you will be able to smell the canning factory.
Pause a moment here, for there
is a fine view across the meadows
to the Castle's ornamental gardens. Turn left
and plough straight ahead stopping for no-one.
Follow the brook up to The Long Wall,
follow the line of the wall westward, and enter
the Castle grounds through The Beggar Gate.
Be sure to shut it after you. There are things
we must keep in, things that have to be protected.
Have your documentation to hand
in case you are stopped by a member of staff.

In Reception you may be given
a blow-by-blow account of domestic strife
in Castle Baden. Alternatively, pick up a leaflet
in the entrance hall, with our compliments.
We have become philosophers since
the blush of virginity left our beds and our lives
became shrubs with more dead wood than living foliage,
and trust our tale will not blight your stay.

When Coleridge stayed here in 1802
he wrote to the effect that his heart was softened
and made worthy to indulge love and
the thoughts that yearn for humankind.
Be that as it may, there are innumerable walks,
and we advise shoes or boots with grip-soles
as the going can often be muddy and slippery.
The village nestles like an irritation
in a fold of land at the north-eastern edge

of the Nameless Hills.
Symbolists come here on field trips;
was the English countryside ever so brilliant?
The history of the village has been written down:
pick up a leaflet in the entrance hall.
There is fine watercolouring to be had
subject to written permission of the owners.

On Thursday evenings Mrs Poole comes in
to play piano, and attendance is obligatory.
We have learned that what we love cannot last,
that if bliss exists at all it is only at the bottom
of a pit of darkness. Mr Poole, dead these fifteen years,
was a great man who refused to trust
the air even when it was in his lungs.

Make the most of your stay here:
flights of incredible fancy increasingly have no place
in this life. Once there was magic.
The first Duke of Baden was able to conjure
a hunting party from the pages of the telephone directory,
his love letters smelled of slowly roasting oxen,
and on top of his wardrobe was a suitcase that had been
all over the Empire. Those days may be gone for ever
but we still have our imaginations.

Now, where are your keys?
Be sure to consider security at all times.
We offer an easy-to-read guide to this
and many other subjects of philosophical enquiry
in a special multilingual format. Pick up a leaflet
in the entrance hall, with our compliments.
Remember, our staff are always on hand to assist.

Finally, please be quiet: we have loved more than our lives
and now try to sleep as much as possible. Notice how
the mind is suddenly clouded but just as suddenly unclouded.

A Hundred of Happiness

Okay. The Finger visits Paris and is entranced by its abandon.
On a river cruiser he falls in love with the notion of The Ripple.
Little does The Finger know that The Ripple has only a short
Time to live, and The Ripple is not used to having a close friend
In whom it can confide its loneliest secrets, its deepest regrets.
The Finger and The Ripple are together in the Parisian summer
And while it lasts there's no point in trying to deny their joy.

Pick of the Films

Adventures in Banking (1989) 6.00 (Channel 5)
    A bank clerk examines his frailties whilst
    buffeted by the delicious breezes of love.
    He expects a cruel wind to sweep him unto
    oblivion. Romantic comedy with a hard edge.

What is Life? (1956) 6.15 (The Kiddy Channel)
    Frederick the Squirrel and Colin the Frog
    foil an international drug smuggling ring
    in this entertaining movie made for children
    using an empty Corn Flakes packet and a piece
    of string.

Climbing Mount Difficult (1986) 9.00 (Channel 14)
    Charles has been likened by his friends to
    an exploding dictionary, but one morning
    he awakens to find that he is become an old man
    chiselling away at a rock face with a teaspoon.
    Psychological drama with Philip Grass soundtrack.

Conjuring Tricks (TV Movie, 1991) 10.30 (Channel 97)
    First in a Brad Cadbury double bill. A seeming
    innocent sleeve is revealed to be harbouring
    a flock of sheep and other weird horrors.
    Classic animation. Followed by

The Hermit (TV Movie, 1991) 11.55 (Channel 97)
    A humble figure stands ready to receive
    the wisest counsel from above, and in turn
    share his deepest wisdom with anyone who needs
    it. Cadbury's masterpiece.

Life Study (1952) 10.45 (Channel 19, black & white)
    Martin seeks a paperweight to hold the thoughts
    he can't fix to his desk or to his paper,

thoughts that blow about on the autumn breeze
with a love beautiful and endless. Comedy
caper starring Bingo Kramer.

The Big Kid (1993) 11.11 (Channel 69)
Dour but compelling, this evocative study of
life as seen through the rear view mirror
of a car parked in woods at midnight won
international acclaim at the 1992 Aldeburgh
Film Festival.

The Longest Five Seconds (TV Movie, 1992) 11.20
(Channel 7)
Separated by nothing more than a million
miles, two lovers talk on the telephone. When
she tells him how much she misses him, there
begins a strange sequence of events that is
bound to end either in disaster or, on the other
hand, fits of hysterical giggling. Riveting
and surprising film shot entirely on location
in the Nottinghamshire coal fields. (Subtitles)

How to Approach a Poem

One way to approach a poem is to disguise yourself
as a slug and hope your mum and dad don't get to hear
how you're letting the family down again. Another way
to approach a poem is to come up on it from behind
and take it by surprise, though this can be dangerous
since many modern poems have equipped themselves
with Reader Warning Devices. One more way to approach
a poem is to ring up and make an appointment
via the poem's receptionist, but this is only any good
if you don't mind waiting a couple of weeks,
and actually the poem you wanted is very busy and
will another one do instead? Another way to approach a
poem is to walk right up to it, put your face in its face
and say, Do you know me? Do I look like someone you know?
Why the fuck are you staring at me then? But this way
can lead to fights, long-term hospitalization and perhaps
even death, so think hard before adopting this method
of approaching a poem. Another way to approach a poem
is to go all gooey-eyed and lovey-duckey over it.
Some people even drool and dribble a bit. This
way works really well but onlookers are likely
to throw up. One more way to approach a poem is to
arrange oneself comfortably in a favourite armchair
by an open fire, set the lights just right, put on
a much-loved CD of classical music at a low volume, and tell
yourself how wonderful you, the poem, and life is. Are.
This is one of the most popular ways of approaching a poem.

Christmas

Something's upset the applecart
and the woman behind the till in the Co-Op
won't stop going on about it.
The queue is building up
and people are beginning to get impatient
but she just won't stop going on
about the applecart and how upset it is.
And I'm stood halfway down the queue
clutching my Cornish pastie and pint of milk
thinking about Christmas and the New Year
and how I wish something would come
along and wipe the next two weeks off
the blackboard of life when
a bloke taps me on the shoulder
and asks me if I've got a gun,
he wants to shoot the woman behind the till
and maybe he'll take out a few others
while he's at it because this is Christmas
and Christmas is all about making people happy
and since he's one of the people
why can't he make himself happy?
So, I give him the gun I've got hidden
in my coat and tell him, Look, it's yours,
keep it, because Christmas is all about giving,
and to give is better than to receive
unless what you receive is better than usual,
like if you are given a knitted swan
and life doesn't mean much to you any more.
And he's so pleased with my gift,
even though it's not wrapped in fancy paper,
that he gets to be in such a pleasant mood
he decides not to kill anybody after all.
Doesn't life just piss you off sometimes?
I mean, that was a pretty decent gun.

Yes

She says that the world is a strange place
and the shops open weird hours, the hours
she is either asleep or on another planet,
and she says she used to believe that all
that could be expected of life was a climb
up a mountain and a scary roll down the
other side, and then she said that her mum
hadn't been the best mum in the world
but as mums go she supposed she wasn't so bad
but there had been moments when things
had got so awful her lack of interest in being alive
had been replaced by a strong desire to be dead,
and then she said she knew loads of people,
all of them men, who really all they wanted
to do was horrible stuff, and if you could
trust anybody in the world they were probably
going to be made of some kind of cloth,
stuffed with foam or cotton wool, and imported
from Taiwan, and then she said that all of
a sudden her life had been turned upside down
and all she could think of was happiness and
all she could think of was brilliant and she
was pretty knocked out by this strange feeling
and should she trust it. Well, should she?

Against Madness

Put a frog in an anthill. Powder the skeleton,
Mix it with bat blood and dried flies, and make it
Into tiny buns. Bake a turtledove, then powder it
And add it to the wine of the woman you desire.
Take a donkey's ear and some oil and boil them
Together. Step upon thy anger with thy heel and
Thy forefoot. Dissolve the brains and heart of a bear
In new wine. Take the gall of a male cat and
The fat of a hen all white, anoint the eyes
And see what others cannot see. Burn the hair
Of a black dog to powder and mix with mother's milk
And child's faeces. May what you see increase
And what you suffer cease. Bake 12 large earthworms
On a shovel and ground to powder. Drink
In a potion. Put black snails in a pot, add salt,
And bury it for nine days. Drink the juice of
Leaves of adder's tongue with distilled
Water of horse tail. Every morning eat a black spider
Between two slices of buttered bread. Anoint your eyes
With gall of cock. Congeal chicken blood
In a small goat's horn. Beat your own shadow with
A cane. Hanker thou after my body, my feet,
Hanker after my eyes, my thighs. Put a blade
Of grass in your mouth and turn to the east.
Fascinate a woman by giving her a piece of cheese.
Put nine drops of your fresh blood on a cloth
In which you will steam the food of the one
You love. ("Every moving thing I have held fast.
Eye and breath I have held fast. I have held fast
All limbs in the deep gloom of night.")
Burn part of a dress after you have
Perspired heavily into it and introduce the ashes
Into the food or drink of the man you desire.
Find a pair of dogs copulating, put a cloth over

Them, and give it to the girl you want. Thread
A needle with her hair and run it through the
Fleshiest limb of a dead man. Piss through
A wedding ring. Spit in your own bosom.
Take milk of a slut and saturate therewith
The spot wherever the hair is desired to grow.
Under a stone that is heavy do we cast thy anger.
Baptize a large toad. Stick pins into a sheep's heart.
Throw hair into the sea to start a storm. Tell your
Bad dreams to the sun. Wear a thumb cover made
From the ear of a black cat boiled in the milk
Of a black cow. At midnight take off your left shoe
And put manure on the big toe. Sit
A naked woman on a heavy stool in the yard.
This is for catching a large fish.

Five Poems

1.
Once upon a time
we could smell the future on the wind.
My mother threw a baby
into the air
and it turned into a dimwit;
he can be seen
in this photograph
trying to bite his elbow.

I take a drop of blood
from the little finger of my left hand
and put it in your drink.
Many waters cannot quench love,
neither can the floods drown it,
for love is strong as death.

2.
The half of everything is so difficult
to understand sometimes:
the eagle's tongue sewn into the collar of a coat,
the rose whose petals fall, portending death.

But I don't think too much about death and miserable stuff:
I do not carry an acorn
in my pocket to stop from growing old,
although if you ask me nicely I will.

Girlie, I'm in a trembling state.
You are the only person in the world
who can make me laugh before breakfast.
Whatever you do, don't go all normal on me.

3.
I want to exercise my opinions like a dog on a staircase
I want to straighten a few things out
I want to put the world and its punctuation in their
                                        proper place
I want to tidy your bedroom as frogs croak in daylight

I hear the melancholy whistling of the golden plover
I see a lone white pigeon on the chimney
I watch ravens fly relentlessly towards one another

I don't understand the half of everything sometimes
I take off all my clothes
I check out myself
I have always been a nervous person
I am prone to stomach problems
I can be a pain on two legs

4.
In this life I have something important to do;
I would love to know what the hell it is.

I write a note to myself,
intending to use it later
as the first line of a short poem
about farm animals:
"My pig can see the wind."

Later, this becomes
"Once upon a time
we could smell the future on the wind",
the opening of a poem that goes on to
misquote *The Song of Solomon*:
Many waters cannot quench love,
neither can the floods drown it,
for love is strong as death.

5.
I awoke last night
and remembered everything
I have ever said
to everybody I have ever met,

but within seconds I'd forgotten the all of it
except one sentence:

"I love you more than these words."

Poem of Carelessness

There is fresh snow on the ground,
it's lying there like flour or washing powder
and I'm too grown up to care about it
or what this weird coloured sky means.

And it's of no consequence to me if a tree
falls on a man's head and knocks him six inches
into the ground like a nail,

or if the wind blows a herd of cows
out of a field into the path of a meat truck
headed for Doncaster
causing death and injury to quite a few people
in ways I don't feel like explaining now.

It's careless when you don't notice
flames licking up your sleeve which is why
you are warm when you thought
it was love's heat coursing through your veins,

and it's careless when you speak out of turn
so a balloon filled with water
bursts from your lips until it explodes
drenching all your so-called buddies.

No. It's of no consequence to me if
the earth freezes over and the sky's canopy
falls on this town like a devastated flower.
The last man to borrow my shoes is
still walking even though the ground long ago
turned to air beneath his feet.

The Secret

To wander aimlessly in a pedestrian precinct
is to do what men without faces have planned for you;
to stride with purpose across a dual carriageway
with no care for the meat lorries and the red cars
is to recognise that your life is more substantial
than metal, more valuable than freight,
and faster than getting somewhere quick.

And when someone flat on their back with the sun
in their eyes tells you it's getting darker by the minute
you know that you are awake and alive in a world
populated by idiots and fools; when the same someone
gets the job you applied for, moves into your house,
persuades your kids to call him Daddy and
he has the keys to your car dangling from his belt
you know he knows something you don't.

Noticing the Wallpaper

I look out the window and notice
how the tree bends in the wind
so it won't break. I notice how
the river winds to avoid the trouble
of climbing hills, and how the railway
bores through the hillside for
the same reason. I notice how the clouds
drift across the face of the sun
so the grass doesn't catch fire, or our
hair, and I notice how they vary in
shape from buffalo to cauliflower,
from subtle brushstroke to reckless daub,
and in colour from white to almost black,
so that looking at the sky is never
boring. Then I notice how green
is never the same colour twice, how
it is not always so green after all,
how it is sometimes brown or red.
And I notice how the tallest trees are not
always the most magnificent, the most
trustworthy or the most honest of men,
and how the smallest bush or shrub
often has plenty to say for itself,
and sometimes it's well worth listening.
I notice the way the fields have been
placed in an interesting patchwork
pattern by unacknowledged hands so
the land looks interesting from the air,
and I notice how the paths and tracks
disappear into the forest and come out
the other side disguised as roads
whose grass verges are home
to countless different kinds of living
creatures, not all of which are
pleasing, or very nice to look at.

The Other Position

How it is under the mother's wing: I'm going to learn to ride a horse before I go to bed and dream of riding on the back of a whale.

How it is under a cloud: I'm going to drink from a cup made from the clay off your boots and let hot oil course through my veins until I glow like a lamp on a windowsill.

How it is under an avalanche: I'm going to rub my thighs with salt from the kitchen cupboard and congratulate myself on the warmth of my stove.

How it is under the waterfall: I'm going to fall in love, argue with myself, and then propose to the girl in the liquid necklaces.

How it is under the full moon: I'm going to run my tongue over your skin and let other men frown in their sleep.

How it is under the cosh: I'm going to bathe my hands in ink and watch the words drip off my fingertips on to the page.

How it is under siege: I'm going to invent machines of sadness and joy and sell them at a massive profit; buy them at your peril.

How it is under observation: I'm going to daub my cock in candle grease and then go look for the matches.

How it is under no illusion: I'm going to set fire to my employer's office and watch the fire brigade at work.

How it is under a lot of self control: I'm going to have six cups of strong coffee, give some stuff a deal of thought, and then retire gracefully.

How it is under a misapprehension: I'm going to have a hot bath, put on my fleecy pyjamas, and go to bed with a good book.

You'd be Better Off Dead

Now, that's unkind.
Nobody deserves that.
Let's be optimistic about the future.
Things aren't as bad as they seem.
There's always someone worse off than you
and though some people have all the luck
things could be worse.
Look, I'd give anything to be in your shoes
and the grass is not always greener
so look on the bright side.
There's always tomorrow,
and tomorrow is another day.

"Gosh, I envy you. You've got it made. You lucky bastard."
That's what he said
and that's what I wrote down afterwards.
That's not how I usually work,
I make up a lot of stuff to be honest,
because I reckon building a world
is as important as dismantling one.

But I don't know what people mean by "lucky".
Remember our discovery of that unheard stanza
from "Stuck Inside of Mobile With The Memphis
               Blues Again",
which would've been worth a fortune
if we'd been able to authenticate it,
but we couldn't so we didn't
and it was another chance gone begging,
one more treacherous carrot dangled,
another chink of light blotted out by reality's lorry.

Note: The stanza, scribbled on the back of a check from a diner out on 61 reads:
"Well the coffee table's dancing like a loaf of bread on dope,

*and the washer's washed its head off and your ice box has lost all hope,
and the neighbours are complaining that you wear some awful clothes
but nothing really matters now because there's nothing left to know."*

But the check has no sure provenance, it could well be a fake, and anyway does this sound like Holy Bob to you? I have my doubts, and doubt is one of the few things I have real faith in these days.

The First and the Last Attempt

He wrote to his mum, a letter enclosed in a parcel that contained a lump of coal painted white, and to his dad he sent an old watch on a gold fob. Upon the vast and windswept plains of his imagination these items symbolised loads, but neither of his parents was ever able to fathom the half of it.

To his brother, he wrote to the effect that there are two kinds of people in the world, but he found it impossible to be either, and to his sister he sent a bunch of flowers in which was concealed an aquatint of a sorry-looking girl adrift upon a brown ocean in an open boat.

To his employer, he scribbled a hasty note: *"A remarkable sea change has burst upon my life, and when you see the rats climbing aboard the ship it's definitely time to take to the skies."*

He let his bank manager know that he was still firm of the opinion that bastards of his order were among the most dedicated of men, and to his various insurers he sent a xeroxed letter, enclosing with each a rose petal that crumbled to dust when the envelope was unsealed.

To the secretary of his Fan Club he mailed a pack containing details of all the places he had never been. Top of the list was Paradise, CA.

To his wife he gave a box of Christmas Crackers and a self-penned pamphlet of acerbic aphorisms entitled "Into The Utmost Unknown". To his children he gave nothing because they already had everything and were in absolutely no danger of losing it.

To his lover he sent his life, and followed it up the motorway in a car he had stolen from outside the local Safeway.

Lies I Must Remember

It wasn't me who forgot to cancel the papers
so the news kept coming and coming and coming.

It wasn't me who ordered
the deep fat fryer from the Kay's catalogue,
setting off the sequence of events
that led to the burning down of our house.

It wasn't me who said
"Love is for ever, and forever is way past my bedtime."

It wasn't me helping the police with their enquiries
into where The Tree of Curiosity had been planted,
and who planted it.
And why.

It wasn't me who noticed that Lust,
passing Beauty on the stair,
tumbleth head over heels like an arse.

It wasn't me who put an elegant chair
leg through the TV screen.

It wasn't me arrested for outrageous handsomeness.

It wasn't me who underwent major surgery
for what doctors described as
"uneven opinions, and too much speaking out loud of
his own mind."

And it wasn't me chalked
CLOUDS OF HAPP
on the sky to show
the marvellous almost in rea

The Wit and Wisdom of Barney Ambrose

In 1972 I lived briefly with
Barney Ambrose, who was famous
around Reading and Slough
for asserting loudly
that one's philosophy is that
upon which one acts,
not that about which one only talks,

in the same way as one's poetic is
what one actually writes,
not what one sometimes claims to write.

People called him The Lip,
and threw mud at his dog, but Barney
would shrug his shoulders and say

"Look, the day glides by,
a chariot of unfulfilled dreams,
but there are more reasons
to be happy than to be sad."

Barney and I would go shopping together
and if I wanted to buy something
but didn't have enough money
he would always lend me some.

I mention all this now because
last night I dreamed that a crowd
stood and stared as my lover
was seduced by a clinical psychologist
with eyes like diamonds

and a great bird of flaming colours
soared unheeded above them,

and I saw myself dangling from its talons
alongside my pal Barney Ambrose

whose voice I could just catch
as it fled on the wings of the wind:

"Martin, look, it's Miranda. It seems like
you're needed if she's not to become
another lost soul. Trust you to be
half a mile up in the air just when
you're needed down on the ground...."

Adventures with Everything

Awakening into daylight the housekeeper daydreams
and becomes a shepherd shepherding
a flock of carpet sweepers sweeping across
the lush green grass of a pasture. The
poet becomes the stone about which he eulogizes,
and the scissors become the event
they are shaping. A paper
bird becomes a black sheet of rain,
astonishing prospects become a dirty mirror
and a worried face becomes an exercise book
filled with algebraic equations.
An explorer in the desert becomes the pyramids
he is looking for, the scientist becomes the last
experiment and everything is revealed.
Night turns into morning, morning into afternoon,
afternoon into evening and evening into night;
daylight into dusk, twilight into darkness into dawn,
and awakening into daylight King Tidy becomes a world
authority on Chaos Theory, the best
laid plans become a pile of bricks
left out in the rain, and the borders
of the kingdom become words on paper.
The mad pianist becomes an astronomer
looking at the moon, the moon becomes a man
whose fortune is made in Heaven,
and a man looking for somewhere
to hide becomes the dark corner.
The card player becomes the Tarot,
and the fool plucks an orange from a tree
as the crowd waits for a lucky card to be handed them
on a plate. Great civilizations pop up
and pop down again as quickly as each page
of The Book of The World is turned,
and coloured balloons on the end of
lengths of twine become newly-discovered planets
upon which life as we know it may or may not exist.

Where Bears Walk

I've been thinking if this is the town
we're going to live in I should tell
my friends what it's like. So friends,
know there are buskers in the market place,
that there is some trading, the sun shines
on the traders as little as it shines on
traders anywhere else in the kingdom,
some intellectual property is exchanged
but not very much, and a deal of idle chatter
falls, leaves drifting down to the pavement
to be trodden underfoot by the inevitable
sports shoe and Doc Marten. Men
and women from distant lands are rare,
the clinking of coin and rustle of paper money
more common, and travellers with tales
to tell pass through but don't stay
very long. Know that the girls' coloured hair
is caught by the sun when it shines
and shines in it, that when business
has been done much remains still to be done
tomorrow, the day after and the day
after that, and that in this as in so many
things this town is the same as
any other. People sit around
wondering what the future might hold
for them, but when a crystal ball
is called for none is forthcoming; the future
will come, someone has written on a wall,
and there's nowt one can do to alter it,
but if a world you imagine is what you know
and love and rest comfortable in the bosom of
then that's fine. This is a state of mind
through which bears walk, but you should know
they are harmless, dogs stand guard
at the wall, and there was a wire fence

separating honesty and deceit but it's been
taken down long since; there was
a well-oiled machinery of men and women
in case of catastrophe
but now all that's needed is friends
you can collapse in the back of.
Only here does music fill the air, only
here do different tongues speak
in many languages and different eyes see
the invisible. Only here is there no lack
of fine sights in the way of birds and beasts,
citizens dressed in white clothes
of good omen, nine times nine white horses
and stars that shine throughout the day.
Know that only here a crowd
gathers to welcome the sun and cheers
like crazy when it catches the girl's
coloured hair, and when the hair flares
the bears walk by her side and they're smiling.

Prince and Princess of Hats

As the morning owes light to the afternoon
because of a day when the Sun refused
to come up over the brow of the hill,
there is something waiting and unfinished,
and when we bought half a knitted hat and a bag of wool
at the Car Boot Sale
we knew we had to see it through,
because we want to be alive and have all our head
and owe it to the other half out of honour.
We've got half a hat that we can work up
into A Great Hat, A Lord of Hats, A King Among Hats,
and there's a day started out at half cock
that can become the best years of our lives. We've got
five pounds that used to be three and which can become
ten if we are sober and industrious, and a hut
to turn into a palace for The Prince and Princess of Hats,
with their feather hats, tree hats,
bonfire hats, jewellery hats,
animal hats, musical hats
and their sprawling city landscape of hats. So,
let's put our heads together
and build a world worthy of all these hats.
When that's fixed, we can invent our own language,
draw our own maps, make our own laws
and start up a club more exclusive than any other.
We can call it The Hat Club.
          People won't like us much
          but we won't care.

Sense of a Horse

The horse broke into the china shop because he mistook
it for a stable. Police enquiries often lead to false arrest.
Perfection is difficult to attain even when aimed for.
A smile graces a girl's face in the evening, but by the time
next morning comes it has been replaced by an expression of
disappointment. If the sun shines on calm lake water it is safe
to take the rowboat out, though be careful not to overload
the food hamper. Perhaps it is best if one of us stays at
home in case the telephone rings. We each have five senses:
sense of guilt, sense of loss, sense of the absurd, sense
of bewilderment and sense of direction. What was going through
the mind of the horse as it was led away by the young constable
cannot be guessed at. Nobody can understand anybody else,
and sometimes it's not worth even having a crack at working
it out. We are able to function in all sorts of different
social situations but are not comfortable in any of them.

Reading the Poem

I read a poem
but don't really get it[1]
and the poet tells me
there's more behind it
than appears
so I go out the back of the poem
to see what's there
but it's just a patch of waste ground
with nothing on it
and nobody around[2]
so I come back in
and have another look
at the front
but it's still tricky there
and getting worse
each time I read it.[3]

The only good thing about this poem
is how the black ink sits
contrastingly on the white paper;
okay, some of the blank spaces
are dead cool,
but that's about it.[4]

Notes
1. I have often been led to believe that there was more to the front of a poem than met the eye, but these experiences only prove that there are those with eyes that seeth that which others cannot see.
2. There are those for whom the front of a poem is the poem, and the back of the poem is the dunghill out of which are raised the needy that they be set with princes.
3. I have lost count of the number of attempts I have made at reading the front of the poem, and would compare it to a wingèd dog with knowledge of many things but no way of telling it to the world.
4. "One must be generous where possible, but not overly so."[5]
5. Stannard, Martin *Conversations with Myself* (unpublished mss)

How I Measure Other People's Lives

I met a man in the late night alchemist's
where I was waiting to get some pills
to replace this dull ache in my stomach
with a sense of purpose and the joys of life,
and he told me about his girlfriend.
He said that he had been laid out half dead
on the beach after being swept off the deck
of a tramp steamer that plied the coast
making a wretched living selling
scavenged goods to poverty stricken
sailors' widows, and she'd revived him
with some magical mutterings. Then,
entering into his heart by way of
the rickety wooden gate at the back,
she'd turned that hard nut into a cherry.
My gosh, I said, you speak of her in an almost
poetic mode. She must be really something.
She is, he replied.
She's like a star above the ocean
and hope in the eye of the sky. When
I'm with her we float away on the wings
of the wind and sail the seas of the moon.
I thought this an exaggeration. The
idea crossed my mind, like the shadow
of magpies at twilight, that I could be talking
to a professional liar, a man
who had dedicated his life to rubbing out
the dividing line between fantasy and fact.
Like most men, I measure other people's lives
by the yardstick of my own experience.

Looking at Maps

I want to visit so many places, but when I go out I always end up on the river bank mis-naming trees, waving to boatmen as they chug by, and looking at ducks. Ducks are okay but they're really only a cheap swan.

Is it nice here? Rugged men hang round outside our door carrying baseball bats. I toss 'em a ball and someone hollers, "Catch it, Joe!" and Joe does, he has a safe pair of hands. Probably they are the biggest hands in the world, and if you are a ball you don't drop out of them and make Joe look a klutz.

Once I was in a restaurant and was very young and my father said we couldn't have any of what we wanted because it was too expensive and he would choose. I always wondered what it would be like to have what we wanted and to get to choose, and the time of day always the morning and the weather sunny and warm.

Book

Title page: *Summer Cloud*. Blank page. Next page: Foreword (to come). Blank page. Next page: Chapter One. Speech marks. Why am I here? Close speech marks. Leave a couple of lines then open speech marks. That's a great question. One of the best. Close speech marks. Next page: Chapter Two. He lit his pipe and sat in the summerhouse looking thoughtful. Next page: Chapter Three. The sun disappeared behind a cloud. Next page: THE END. Blank page. Next page: Notes (to come). Next page: Notes on further reading (to come). Next page: Biographical note on author (to come). Next page: By the same author: *Spring Tears, Autumn Leavings, Winter Fires, A Life in Weather* (all to come).

Life of Fish

He kisses her incessantly and sometimes they forget to eat,
such is the sea of bliss in which they swim.
Only when the Sun pulls itself awake from its slumbers
do they look up and pause
to take a break from what has turned from a hobby into a career,
and to go through the pile of mail that has gathered about them
    like a fog-bank in February.
She cuts the envelopes open with her fingernails
and he rips the letters to shreds with his wit and funny
    comments.
They do this as quickly as possible,
although sometimes their laughter makes their tummies hurt
    and they have to rest.
Then he takes up kissing her again,
and they are still kissing when the Sun dips down into the
    night's water
and the only noise to break the silence of their joy
is the sound of the ocean breaking upon some rocks.

Punish

Postcards from seasides abroad make us happy
for the people who sent them,
they are having fun and sun in a hot place
and they deserve it
for being sober and industrious all the rest of the year.
We, on the other hand, have not been very good
and are being punished for our crimes:
when we wake up in the morning the sun is not shining,
no visitors come to the house to brighten the day
and we are unable to go out because
we have had our sense of direction taken away from us
so when we go anywhere beyond the back gate
we wind up very lost.
Oh please let us have our sense of direction back
and please remove these dull grey clouds from our lives!
We have forgotten exactly what it was we did wrong,
it was all so long ago,
but surely we have been punished enough,
and we are aching to go to the new adventure park
where we will be free
to act like brainless idiots on dope
and blend innocuously into the crowd.

The Aeroplane

Mr Wind pursing his lips
and blowing horribly horizontal
as we walk the hill and the sky
lowering on to our heads
like a hat. Now the rain
falling in lumps and our clothes
hanging on us like wet rags.
Running for home and tumbling
headlong into the grass
and coming up for air with our head
bleeding. Laughing like a criminal
because an upside down person
suffering from mild concussion
and wet as a fish is
very funny if it's not you.
Carry me home like unto a funeral
and cleanse my wounds with balm.
All right. But before we go,
look: a rainbow over the hilltop,
and an aeroplane
following its curve.

Martin Stannard was born in 1952, and has been publishing and performing his poetry since 1977. He was the founding editor and publisher of *Joe Soap's Canoe* poetry magazine (1978 – 1993). He has worked extensively in community arts and in community and adult education, and regularly teaches writers' workshops. He has also held a number of writing residencies, including work with mosaic artist Arik Halfon on a village trail in Bassingham, Lincolnshire. His reviews of poetry feature regularly in a number of magazines. He lives in Newstead, near Nottingham.

Other books by Martin Stannard
Half Man Half Hammock Half Marlo Brandon (Syntaxophone 1979); *The Private Life of the Gauze Butterfly* (Kawabata 1980); *The Lotte Poems* (Torture Books 1981); *Baffled in Nacton* (Greylag Press 1983); *The Flat of the Land* (Wide Skirt Press 1987); *Something Cold and White* (Bad Seed 1987); *The Gracing of Days: New & Selected Poems* (Slow Dancer 1989); *Denying England* (Wide Skirt Press 1989); *Easter* (Waldean Press 1994). Poems have also appeared in a variety of anthologies, including *High On The Walls* (Bloodaxe).

Smith/Doorstop Books

publish books, cassettes and pamphlets by

Moniza Alvi
Simon Armitage
Sujata Bhatt
Liz Cashdan
Julia Casterton
Linda Chase
Debjani Chatterjee
Bob Cooper
Tim Cumming
Peter Daniels
Carol Ann Duffy
Anna Fissler
Katherine Frost
John Harvey
Jo Haslam
Geoff Hattersley
Jeanette Hattersley
Keith Jafrate
Mimi Khalvati
John Lancaster
Peter Lane
John Lyons
Ian McMillan
Cheryl Martin
Eleanor Maxted
David Morley
Les Murray
Dorothy Nimmo
Pascale Petit
Lemn Sissay
Joan Jobe Smith
Martin Stannard
Mandy Sutter
Mary Woodward
Cliff Yates